NASA

Julie Murray

Abdo Kids Junior
is an Imprint of Abdo Kids
abdobooks.com

Abdo
US SYMBOLS
Kids

abdobooks.com

Published by Abdo Kids, a division of ABDO, P.O. Box 398166, Minneapolis, Minnesota 55439.
Copyright © 2020 by Abdo Consulting Group, Inc. International copyrights reserved in all countries.
No part of this book may be reproduced in any form without written permission from the publisher.
Abdo Kids Junior™ is a trademark and logo of Abdo Kids.

Printed in the United States of America, North Mankato, Minnesota.

052019

092019

THIS BOOK CONTAINS
RECYCLED MATERIALS

Photo Credits: Getty Images, iStock, NASA, Shutterstock

Production Contributors: Teddy Borth, Jennie Forsberg, Grace Hansen

Design Contributors: Christina Doffing, Candice Keimig, Dorothy Toth

Library of Congress Control Number: 2018963320

Publisher's Cataloging-in-Publication Data

Names: Murray, Julie, author.

Title: NASA / by Julie Murray.

Description: Minneapolis, Minnesota : Abdo Kids, 2020 | Series: US symbols |
    Includes online resources and index.

Identifiers: ISBN 9781532185373 (lib. bdg.) | ISBN 9781532186356 (ebook) |
    ISBN 9781532186844 (Read-to-me ebook)

Subjects: LCSH: National Aeronautics and Space Administration--Juvenile
    literature. | Astronautics--United States--Juvenile literature. | Outer space--
    Exploration--Juvenile literature.

Classification: DDC 354.790973--dc23

Table of Contents

NASA

NASA is the US space agency.

It was started in 1958.

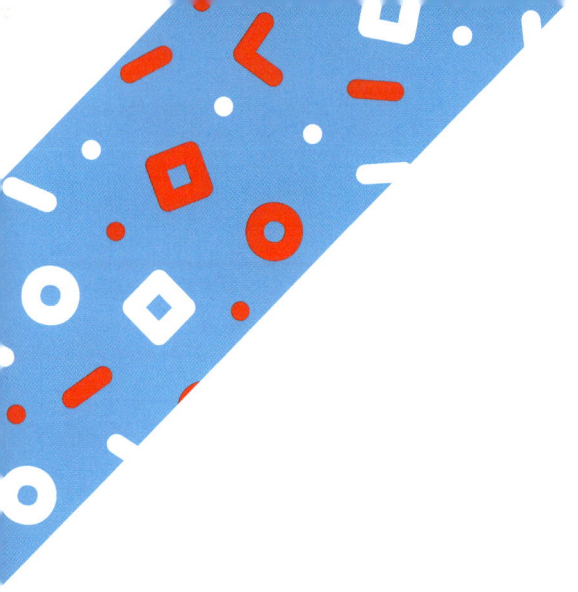

They study space. Anne works

in a space lab.

They explore it too! They sent a **rover** to Mars!

Many people work on Earth. Tracy works at the **control center**.

Some work in space.

Dan does a spacewalk.

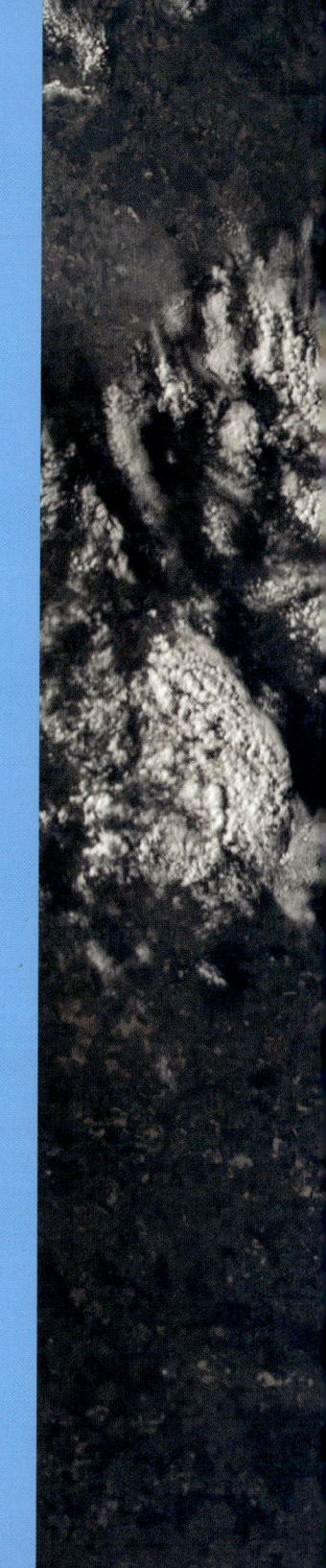

They take pictures. They look at moons. They look at **galaxies** too!

They learn about planets.

Saturn is a big ball of gas.

It has rings.

NASA landed on the moon!

It was in 1969.

The NASA Seal

blue sphere for
exploring planets

stars for
exploring space

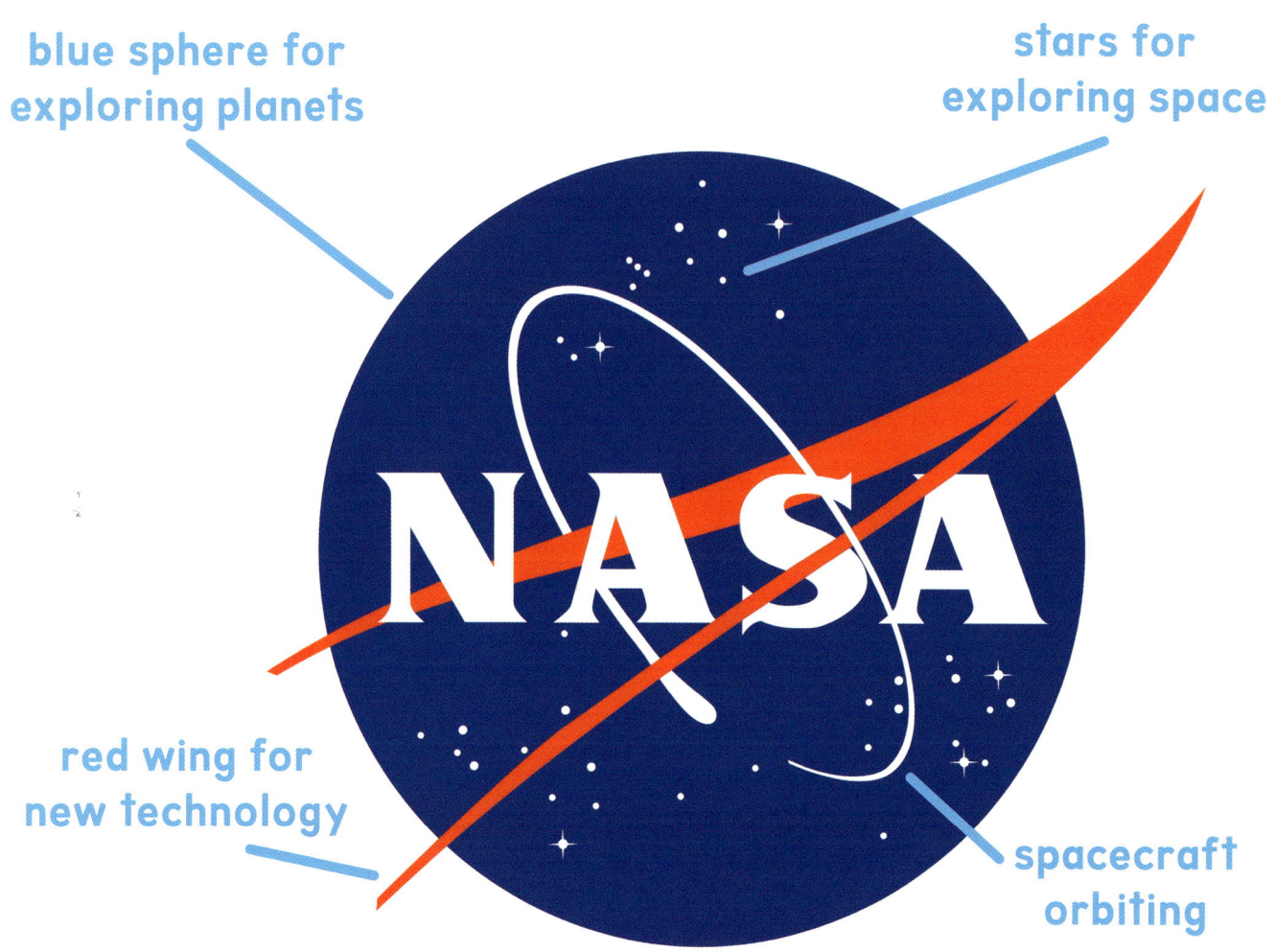

red wing for
new technology

spacecraft
orbiting

Glossary

galaxy
a collection of billions of stars and other matter held together by gravity.

rover
a type of vehicle designed to travel on a planet, comet, or moon.

control center
a place on Earth that manages space flights from launch to landing.

23

Index

Abdo Kids ONLINE FREE! ONLINE MULTIMEDIA RESOURCES

Visit **abdokids.com** to access crafts, games, videos, and more!

Use Abdo Kids code

UNK5373

or scan this QR code!